# Pineapple Flowers

Karel Ensing

Presentation by *BookLeaf Publishing*

Web: www.bookleafpub.com

E-mail: info@bookleafpub.com

ISBN: 978-93-5744-979-3

First edition 2022

# CONTENTS

# Leipziger

I.

The snow falls slowly
On the snow-covered streets
Of Leipzig.

And the room you share
With the lady from Hong Kong
At the space hotel.

The insistent smells
Of the strange foods she keeps
On the balcony.

And the puffed-up sparrows
Chirping
In a park.

Where a young boy
Drinks beer, lights a cigarette
Awaits the summer.

And the man on the other side of the street
Who, if only for a moment,
Mistook you for someone else.

The children sliding down slopes
On sleds made of wood.
Surrounded by trees that could be anywhere in
Europe.

And the graffiti on the statues
Of fallen angels
At the Hochschule für Grafik und Buchkunst.

The young mothers strolling with their newborns
As white, as innocent,
As silent as snow.

The way people stamp
Their feet
Before entering a building.

All this seems very welcoming.

II.

As I Imagined her sitting
At the small round kitchen table.
A black kitten sleeping
In the palm of her hand
I wondered,
Does a blind man
Close his eyes
Upon sleeping?

On my knees at her feet
I stroked the kitten's knitted brow
Feigning interest in the young unseeing thing
As an excuse to fleetingly touch
Her naked palm
Soft and warm
Her fingers
Full of splinters
From working on the bulwarks.

When suddenly the kitten
Walked across my arms
To rest its small paws
On my left shoulder.

For a moment I thought
Of opening the eyes of the kitten.
Changing its view of the world
Beyond repair.

A fitting punishment
For its treachery.

III. (I'm in your room opening a window)

I'm in your room (like a womb
Hoping to pick up some words
Looking for loot
Careful not to leave a mess
Erasing all traces
Watching my palms grow
Sensing how my temples are formed
Still in touch with the thoughts
Of she who carries me
I know she fears
This time it will be too late
But I am convinced myself
Whenever I go
It will be too soon)

Opening a window.

IV.


Even with all its empty buildings,
With the debris, broken glass, sharp stones,
The thorny fruits she brings forth,
Even with the splintered windowsills of
abandoned homes,
On a good summer day,
You can still see young girls,
Strolling barefoot,
On the streets of Leipzig.

V.

I think my feet have taken a liking
To the sidewalks of Wedding.
It is almost as if I know where I'm going.

But not just my feet, my thoughts too
Wrapped in thin layers of glass
They don't mind to be shattered.

Not just my thoughts, Bernard too
Without saying a word he left the electrical box
That held our drinks and elbows

For a moment I thought he would take off
But heavy with dance
As if already translated

Into stone he fell down
Leaving a little stain of blood
Next to the unharmed bottle of beer

Still warm from his grasp.

VI.

A woman collecting
The seeds from the purple
Flowers surrounding
The bronze statue
In Friedenspark.

Saving them
In a little white envelope
To give to her grandchildren,
To sow in her garden,
The corner of her street

The wrappings around the Russian church,
The kites caught in the trees,
Fluttering in Protest,
"When you were born all this was still a
cemetery!"

VII.


Mary!
You've come back
With different eyes
A different voice
Speaking a different tongue
But by God,
The very same ears!

Mary!
After seven months
You've come back
Without the scars
On your ankles, wrists, temples
But by God
I'll find other places to kiss

Mary!
After seven months
You've come back from the dead
With the same tempered breath
The same sick air filling your lungs
But by God
Pass me by
Without as much as a word of thanks
As if unaware
It was my longing
That brought you back.

VIII.

Fighting for the knife,
O how they like to cut vegetables!

Put your ear to the Pentax,
Yes it still works!

Take a picture of the girls
Dancing in cotton dresses
Three red candles in each hand!

IX. - for Farina -


I said to her, (or wish I had said)
'You know
When I was young
I wanted to be a baker.'


[Thinking,
I became part of a City
Ridden with empty buildings.]


Saying (or wishing I had said,)
'Because I was always up so early
It only seemed convenient.


Of course as I grew up
I woke up later and later
And the dream waned'


[Thinking,
And high up
One of its humbled walls,
Found a little flower
Growing against all odds.]


Saying (or wishing I had said,)
'But now...'

[Thinking,
What color!
What vigor!]

...'I think this old passion
Has taken a hold of me again.'

[Thinking,
I love you indefinitely.]

X.

So I told her about the abyss
And put in words it seemed a pit.
I told her about the dirt, the dark cold ground
That used to cover it.

I said: "I've felt so lost"
(But unlike the loss that seems to rid
This language of a deeper love,
A theory a thought it is.

A longing twisted by a tongue
That never keeps its grasp, not fit
To speak my mind, distorted by
A body full of lies!)

I always thought " 'tis a lost cause
No shovel can fill her, still the hunger of the pit.
No hands bring back the man
I have tried so hard to miss."

But now I say: "This abyss,
These words turned into a pit,
Let's dig her out, let's pitch the pit,
Let's build a valley,
Have her past smeared out so far
You can almost see through it.

Let's fill her up with water,
Have the young deer drink,
The tree roots sap, the lotus bloom in it.
And bathe ourselves, cleanse the histories.
Wash the words from off the paper.
Change our skin and swim
As far as it can take us."

XI.


I saw two boys
Staring at a red ball
Stuck in a tree

So I picked up some rocks
And threw them at the branches

After many a missed attempt
Finally,
With a soft thud,
As if it too sighed in relief,
The ball came


Loose


All three of us broke out in cheers
But after our triumph waned
And we were strangers again,
Separated by a language
And twenty years between us,

I thought,
Why have I stopped throwing
Rocks at the well

Kept silent machine on my desk


Why have I stopped my fingers
From falling on her keys
Made an effort
To rid myself
Of every opportunity
To strike a perfect chord:

A series of words
Describing thoughts
I had no idea
Were boiling deep inside of me
With unfathomable clarity.

XII.

I watch her as she
Cuts the ginger roots and carrots
In even slices,
Fries the shrimp,
Rinses the rice
Till the water runs clear.

I see her tired but beautiful face
See her slow measured movements
And suddenly realize
That, even though
(Among other feats of courage)
I would chow down whole
Apple chores as a young boy
This does not mean
(No matter what they told me)
That if you cut me open
At this very moment
You would find
The blossoming branches
Of an apple tree.

When I read this to her
She will say:
"That's not true!
I did not cut them in even slices
In fact, I did not even cut the carrots
You did!
And what's the deal
With that apple tree?
For all its blossoms
I don't want its branches
This is not the poem you promised me!"

To which I will reply:
Darling you are interrupting me again.
All I had left to say was...
"But it's a lie!"
You are right but you see it's a poem
It needs to fit the rhythm
I have to be concise.

"And what's with the apple tree?"
It stands for all the dormant thoughts
I never cared to discard
And poses the question
How to fill the empty space
After they are spirited away.

"You are talking about God again, aren't you"
It's not important
What I wanted to tell you
Is that I've come to hunger
For both you and your sushi
I long for your pho soup
But God knows how much I want to
Carry you to the bedroom
(Let the water boil
I don't care if the walls turn black)
And make love to you.

# Big Words

In the waiting room
I was coughing like a madman
All morning

The first thing the doctor said
after she called me in was

"I could hear you from here!"

Her eyes said
"All my years of training. For this?"
But her lips said

"Open your mouth,
I want to have a look inside."

I obliged and wished
There was a way
I could have a look myself

She only needed a few seconds.

Then she said
"Just what I expected "

Taking the stethoscope from my chest
"Yes, it all adds up"

If memory serves me well
She even snapped her fingers
Triumphantly when she said

"Sir you have the severest case
Of b i g  w o r d s  I have ever seen."

"To be honest,
With something of that magnitude
Growing in your throat
I don't know how you
Still manage to breathe
Let alone speak!
The itch must kill you!"

I nodded and wanted
To ask what could be done
But had to break off mid-sentence
Due to another coughing fit

She gave me a prescription
And ordered me
To get the pills
As soon as possible.

But walking me to the door
She whispered,

"Back there I was just
Talking to you as a doctor.
As a romantic
I implore you,

Let them ripen!
Let them grow so heavy
It only takes a gust of wind
To let them fall
in the tall grass below!"

"What a wondrous thing
To see words
As big as this
Cramped together in a human mouth!
And at the same time
What a pity
their size prevents us
From reading them."

I stood in front of the pharmacy
For almost an hour
Dawdling
In the end I did not go inside

Instead of getting the pills
I went home and
Bought a cheap flight to London,

The rainiest city
I could think of,
And rambled her streets
For two days
From dawn till dusk
Wearing nothing but a pair of jeans
An old t-shirt
And an open jacket

# Changing Seats

I.

The seats in the boarding area
Are strikingly similar
To the seats
In the doctor's office

But it is not me who sees this
This time it is you
At the airport

I am at home
And no matter what I do
My eyes won't open

(I only know this
Because it is something
I learned to count on)

II.

Not being able
to open my eyes
I see you
Standing in line
To get on your flight
Thinking:

This river I leave behind
When I come back
Will have changed beyond recognition

III.

I wish I could
Stop this train of thought
Drown out the
Public announcements the
Gate changes the
Remove all metal items
From your clothing and body
And take off your shoes the
Last chance to boards and
Let you know

IV.

I was hoping
You, who learned
To swim in wild waters
At the prime age of three,
Would be aware
That, yes

Maybe the river
Is always a different river

And the swimmer
Swimming in the river
Always a different swimmer,

But you still need to float
To keep your head above the water

And if a current pulls you under
All of this nitpicking
No longer seems important

You will not question
How long it has been there

You will struggle to
Get to the surface

V.

And sometimes
you need a helping hand
To get pulled out

And like the current
You don't question the hand

# Pineapple Flowers

If, when you come back
Your blood enriched
With oxygen taken from
The purest mountain air,
Spreading a fresh scent
Of pineapple flowers,

Strong enough
To overwhelm whatever
Makes ascending your staircase
Seem like opening
A hundred cans
Of cat food,

(Something we previously
Thought was impossible) if,
Upon entering your room,
The first thing you look at
Is the very same empty
Bottle that toppled
Over on that glorious day,

Leaving the top shelve
Of your half empty bookcase,
Intent on gaining a felicitous velocity
Enough to strike a blow
And reach

The water table of my love.
Or if it's gone
Look at the empty spot.
This will do, no more would be needed
To help me through
The last days of our separation.

# Green Leaves

Right now I could say it.
But of course there are times
When I'm less elated
When all words, all keys
Are long lost or hidden

And when sought for when caught
Who knows what bycatch
We'll find twisting in the nets

And when we set them
Free from their traps
Who knows if
They'll leave my mouth withered
With flaglike grey flutters
Or turn out to be

The first fresh green leaves
That sudden release
Of springtime

Yes there are times
I just can't say it
But you see
That's when I try
To stay as far away from
My writing table as possible

That's not what I want to remember

# Like Snow

There's not a lot left
I wish there was
But there's not a lot left

Just this bright light
That keeps me up at night

Just this silence
You can feed anything

Just the traces of your hands
Your face on mine fading

When the snow melted
I too felt I should take back
Everything I had said

It was this reversed insatiability
That made me leave my bed
And walk to the Mariannenpark
In the middle of the night

That led me up the little hill
Where I stood long enough to believe
I had more or less become
The absent darkness
Of an ink blot
That part of the night
Where surrender is gathered

Wrapped in soot and shadows
I started snowing again
Till day broke

# Love or Life loaded Die

The first anxiety
Has waned. How few words
It took for her
To calm you down.

Now grown audacious
Brazen-faced we hear you say:

"From now on
All existential worries
Will be nothing to me
For once you've played this game
With love loaded die

(Perhaps love larger than life loaded die
Or, who knows, love of a life loaded die)

And kept your calm

Mere life loaded die
Can't do you harm"

We stand there uneasy
And laugh with a laugh
Of hope wrapped in ridicule

# So far away. So far

You so far away
So far I've written
And remained unnoticed

But soon you
Will unmask
The poems above
For what they are

You so far away
So far I have believed
In one universe

But now I've seen
The multiplications and the splintering

You so far away
So far there is
One universe in which you will say
"How dare you involve me into this"

But another in which you will
Softly whisper "John"
Or any of the other names you gave me

And yet another universe where saying:
"One month has passed
It will be easier from now on"
Is enough for it to be thus
This will be enough

You so far away
So far you've yet to notice
How I twist your words
To make them fit here

And when you do
I hope you can
Find it in your heart
To forgive me

Remember,
It was our rocking that made the bottle shake
then topple
It is you who makes me dream
Of pineapple flowers

It is both your hands and mine
That spell the words
Then let them swarm from tongue to lips
Then back, then loose and off
And here it is
one side of a cosmic kiss
Waiting for an answer

# Valparaiso

How fitting
For you to be
In a beautiful city

To sit at
Neruda's desk
And look out
over the harbour

If he was still around
He would write you down
If I was there
I would kiss you all over

Call me up
And tell me more
About Valparaiso

# Recipe

Here it is:

Mix 50 grams of oats,
100 grams of rye flour,
200 grams of wheat flour,
And an equal amount of longing
In a large bowl
Add a pinch of salt and a little bit of sugar
Make sure to mix it well
with the oats and the flour
Before adding the yeast
and everything you miss about her
Because if the yeast gets
in direct contact with the salt
The dough won't rise.
Take a small carrot,
An onion of about the same size
And if you are brave enough
A slip of paper.
Grate the carrot,
Dice the onion,
fill the paper with b i g  w o r d s,
The ones that have been itching
In your throat for so long
(Even more so now she's gone),

Shred the paper to pieces
And fold all of it in.
Measure 250 milliliters of water
And add it sip by sip
Stirring the mix with a spoon after each sip.
Leave about 20 milliliter for the plant
The one that hung her head
The first time she came over
But has now grown strong and tall
Fresh leaves showing every time you look at it.
Let the dough slip on a flour dusted board
Knead till it's somewhat elastic.
Let it rise for 30 Minutes.
Turn on the oven.
Look at the picture of her
And her cat named Vodki.
Knead the dough. Let it rise again.
Put it in the oven for 40 minutes.
Spread butter luxuriously.
Sprinkle with sunflower seeds.
Then eat.

Repeat the next day

# Apricot Tree

I stepped back
One step
And out of the dappled chaos of colour
A face appeared a

Naked
Body slowly
Dressing

Now that it had come to life
The picture started moving
By its own volition

I stared at her baffled
As she left the museum

As she went south
And still became clearer

As she flew across the ocean
Still taking on shape

As she arrived in her hometown
Finally full-fledged

Yes, as you stood there
By the apricot tree
Planted in your youth
Various shoots around her now
And everything in bloom
I knew

Yes, as you took
A step back
Taking in the smell,
That's when I knew that

Underneath the thick layer
Of my imagination
With you I would find
The rich earth
Of a life full of love

# I am a Gathering

At noon I am two girls
Talking in the thin shade
Of a broken lamppost
Laughing
At night I am both
The flickering light
And the single star
My flickering light
Drowns out

Right now
I am a woman
Slowly picking empty
Beer and soda cans
From a bin one by one
But I just as much
Am the last drops
Of these cans
Splattered on the flagstones

Later I'll turn into the air that is
Trapped in the cans
And when we're suddenly
Thrown on a pile
I'm the cans themselves
Begging for mercy
But if it cannot be avoided
I'll happily be
The sound of the cans
Being crushed on the pavement

Because I am the waves behind us
And the unforgiving sun above
I am also the man
Sitting on the steps
Of the church
Whetting a knife
And for the same reason
I am the knife
Waiting to be sharp again
At times I'm sure
I am the whetting stone too
And the fruit, and the flesh
And the thoughts we'll cut open

But then again
Am I not the man
Painting his face
In the shade of an orange tree?
A bouquet of plastic flowers
Hidden in the left sleeve
Of a worn out jacket?
Yes! I am the juggling of cones
At the traffic lights
And, who would doubt it,
The hands we hold up,
The path we wear out in the asphalt

I am a long working day
A band of street dogs barking
A stand dressed with skeletons
Carved out of driftwood

I am three coconuts left
To the mercy of the waves
And feeling just as lost
I am the net that
Hauls us to the shore

I am the winding road to the canyon
The voice that says 'amigo'
And the eyes that answer 'yes -
But no - but why -
We've never met'

I am a street food vendor
spitting in his hands,
I am the tattooed swastika
On the right arm of the
Smiling tricycle driver
Showing us the way
To the waterfalls

I am the stones of mayan temples
And the cathedral built above it
I am a hundred plastic bottles
Eight left and ten right flip flops
Gathered together on the shore

I am the tequila
That fills the mouths
Of the friends of the groom
I am the agave plant
That waited fifteen years
To bring this joy
I am the pearl white
dress of the bride
Suddenly drenched in wine
Mixed with spite

I am the tree roots
Breaking through
The cement of
A dusty park's pathway
Sprinkled with purple blue,
White pink and bright red petals

I am the girl tickling
Her abuela waiting
For the next bus
To Acapulco
I am don Pulpo
Getting drunk in the morning
Knee deep in the surf
Of the grey water of Progreso

I am a stray jungle dog
Licking his wounds
On top of a pyramid
Baffling the tourists
As they bend over to
Catch their breath
After the steep climb up

I am the dew on the yellow
Pineapple flowers
The relief fresh cut sabila brings
To hot sunburnt skin
I am the flesh
Of a red ripe papaya
I am a cactus grown man high
I am her twists and turns
Towards the sun

I am a gathering of
All of the above
Because the same hands
That weave the hammock
That rock the baby
Tune the guitar
Untune the guitar
Only so they can tune the guitar again

Gesture a wish to stay
And a longing to come back

# Gods

I.

After we talked
all through the night

I staggered to bed drunk

And woke up full of God
s

II.

Wondering
Isn't it worth considering
That out of this vast forever darkness
Despite the odds,
Life
would rear its head
Its voice still wet
with nothingness
Staggering at the door
On thin doe legs
Pleading for more
Ladling up starry milk
with a nimble tongue

Should we not
at least mention
That out of life
We can spin mellifluous thought?

And out of thought
we can wring language
And out of language
We can create beauty?

And out of beauty
We can grow love
And is there love
That does not speak?

Or words robust enough
To stand alone
That do not attract others
So as to happily
Sift through the cracks

And form these little piles
These silent voids bearing witness that
Out of language
We can create thought

And out of thought
We can escape into life
And on top of life
We can spread out
A thin layer of fiction
And in this fiction
There is wiggle room
For an innocent God
Putting flowers in a vase
At a kitchen table
Singing a universe into being

III.

I know in any other given situation
I would have done the same
And spared you the trouble

The roles
Could have been reversed
Easily. After all
This is how we were brought up

Tainted with a stubbornness
That led our grandparents
To start a new church
In the middle of a war

We, with the same tenacity
Running through our veins,
Break it down
Stone by stone

Now you wag your callous
fingers over my soft beating chest
As I try to pour
This quivering storm,
This incomprehensible complexity
This all encompassing, staggering beauty

Into a marmalade jar
fissured and dusty,
Into a discarded envelope
Ripped open carelessly,
Into a small palimpsest receptacle;
this treacherous word
God

Tomorrow I'll tell you
These attempts are doomed to fail

But now...
What visions!
What intimations!
What wonderful splinters
Are stuck in my fingers!
Feel them!
Are not the velvet calluses
On my hands
Proof enough?

Why make little of
My reader's appreciation
For this intricate fabric
so carelessly spun
by time?

IV.

Waking up from
A series of
Whirling dervished dreams
It suddenly comes to me:

I should have memorized
A few lines of Alberto Caeiro
For anyone in need of
A new appreciation of life

# Will we Well up

Will we well up
While we wait
At the station
If in May or in April
Will we well up
In September
While we wait
For the other
If a friend
Or a lover
From a long forgotten summer
Or a past
With a weight
That you carry
With you always

Will we well up
At the station
In October
Or a cold November morning
We arrived,
Of course, too early
And the hours
Progress so slowly
That with every other train

Yes, with each
Unfamiliar face
That looks away,
We wonder
Did we waste
Another day?

Will we well up
When the other
Be it August or December
Leaves the train
With Abandon
Scans the platform
Sees us standing
As we wait
As our eyes meet
Will we well up
Thinking, surely,
You are different
But the same